The Jungle Book
Rudyard **Kipling**

Illustrated by **Paolo D'Altan**
Adapted by **Kelly Reinhart**
Activities by **Eleanor Donaldson**

© 2007 D Scuola SpA
Via Privata Mondadori, 1 – 20054 Segrate (MI)
First edition: January 2007

We would be happy to give you further information concerning our material and receive your comments.

info@blackcat-cideb.com
blackcat-cideb.com

Editor: Michela Bruzzo
Design and art direction: Nadia Maestri
Computer graphics: Simona Corniola
Illustrations: Paolo D'Altan
Picture research: Laura Lagomarsino

DEALINK, DEAFLIX are trademarks licensed by
De Agostini SpA

Picture credits:
© Bateman's, East Sussex, UK / National Trust Photographic Library /John Hammond / The Bridgeman Art Library: 4

All rights reserved. No part of this book may be reproduced, stored in a retrieval system or transmitted, in any form of by any means, electronic, mechanical, photocopying, recording or otherwise, without the written permission of the publisher.

CISQ CERT
TEXTBOOKS AND TEACHING MATERIALS
The quality of the publisher's design, production and sales processes has been certified to the standard of
UNI EN ISO 9001

Reprints
10 9 8 7 6 5 4 3 2 1
2031 2030 2029 2028 2027 2025

Printed in Italy by Italgrafica srl – Novara

Contents

About the Author — 4

CHAPTER **ONE** Mowgli's Family — 7

CHAPTER **TWO** Council Rock — 16

CHAPTER **THREE** Lessons with Baloo — 23

CHAPTER **FOUR** Kaa — 31

CHAPTER **FIVE** The Lost City — 39

Let's meet some of the animals in the story! — 46

CHAPTER **SIX** Kaa's Dance — 50

CHAPTER **SEVEN** The Red Flower — 59

CHAPTER **EIGHT** Tiger! Tiger! — 67

India — 75

UNDERSTANDING THE TEXT   12, 20, 28, 36, 44, 56, 64, 74

Special Features:

KET KET-style activities   12, 20, 22, 28, 29, 36, 44, 45, 49, 56, 74

T: GRADE 2   Trinity-style activities (Grade 2)   14, 30, 66

PROJECT ON THE WEB — 76
Exit Test — 77
Key to Exit Test — 80

   These symbols indicate the beginning and end of the passages linked to the listening activities.

Rudyard Kipling (1891) by John Collier.

About the Author

Name: Rudyard Kipling
Born: 30 December 1865 in Bombay, India
First book of short stories: *Plain Tales from the Hills* (1888)
Most famous book: *The Jungle Book* (1894)
Other books: *The Second Jungle Book* (1895), *Captains Courageous* (1897), *Kim* (1901), *Just So Stories* (1902)
Prizes: Nobel Prize for Literature (1907)
Travels: England, United States, South Africa, India
Dies: 18 January 1936 in London, England

BEFORE YOU READ

1 VOCABULARY

Look at the picture. Match the words below with the animals and the things in the picture. Can you find all the words in three minutes?

1 cave
2 rock
3 wolf pack
4 cub
5 pebbles
6 jungle
7 tiger
8 moon

2 VOCABULARY – ANIMALS

Do you know these animals? Label the pictures with the correct word, like in the example (0).

snake   bird   bull   ~~panther~~   frog
bear   monkey   jackal   wolf

0 panther
1
2
3
4
5
6
7
8

CHAPTER ONE

Mowgli's Family

One evening in the hills of south India, Father Wolf wakes up. Mother Wolf is near him with four little cubs.

'It's time to look for food,' says Father Wolf. He gets up and leaves the cave. There is a big moon in the sky.

'Hello!' says a voice. It is the jackal Tabaqui. He eats everything, even old clothes from the villages. The wolves do not like him and are afraid of him.

'What do you want, Tabaqui?' asks Father Wolf.

'The tiger Shere Khan is coming here to look for food,' says Tabaqui.

'What!' says Father Wolf, surprised. 'He can't do that. He must tell us first because that's the Law of the Jungle.'

'Shere Khan has a bad leg and he can't run fast,' says Mother Wolf. 'He only kills bulls, and the people of the village are angry with him. That's why he's coming here. He wants to start hunting[1] in a new place.'

'Listen!' says Tabaqui. 'You can hear him in the woods.'

---

1. **hunting** : killing animals for food.

THE JUNGLE BOOK

Father Wolf listens and says, 'What a stupid animal! He's making a lot of noise and all the animals are going to run away and hide. How can I look for food now?'

'Shhh,' says Mother Wolf. 'It's the noise of a... man!'

'A man!' cries Father Wolf.

The Law of the Jungle says that animals must not eat man, because then a lot of men with guns [1] come to the jungle. And all of the animals are in danger.

'Listen!' says Mother Wolf. 'Something's coming to the cave.'

Father Wolf sees a baby standing under a tree. The baby looks at Father Wolf and laughs.

'Is that a man cub?' asks Mother Wolf. 'Bring it here; I want to look at it.'

The baby is small and has no clothes. Father Wolf gently carries it to Mother Wolf. It starts drinking her milk with the other cubs.

Mother Wolf is happy and says, 'Look, he's drinking my milk with the cubs. He's not afraid.'

It is suddenly dark in the cave because Shere Khan puts his big head inside.

'We're pleased to see you, Shere Khan,' says Father Wolf, but his eyes are angry.

'I know there's a man cub here,' says Shere Khan. 'It's mine! You must give it to me!'

'Shere Khan's very big so he can't come into the cave,' thinks Father Wolf.

'The man cub is ours,' says Father Wolf. 'The leader of the pack's going to decide what to do with the cub. We listen to him and not to a tiger.'

1. **guns** :

'The man cub is mine!' cries Shere Khan angrily. He starts roaring.¹

'No!' cries Mother Wolf. 'The man cub is mine and you can't kill him. He's going to live with us. He's my son! Now go away!'

Shere Khan walks around the cave slowly and looks at the man cub.

'No, I'm Shere Khan, and the cub is mine.'

'You're wrong,' says Mother Wolf. 'The man cub is ours. He's going to live with us. He's my son! Now go away, Shere Khan.'

Father Wolf is surprised, but he knows Mother Wolf is brave² and strong.

1. **roaring** : making the sound tigers make.   2. **brave** : not afraid.

Shere Khan goes away. He knows he cannot fight [1] Mother Wolf in the cave. 'One day I'm going to have that cub!' he cries.

After Shere Khan leaves, Father Wolf says, 'Do you really want to keep him?'

'Yes, I do,' says Mother Wolf. 'He isn't afraid of us and he's happy here. I want to call him Mowgli the frog.'

'Mowgli?' says Father Wolf. 'Yes, I like the name Mowgli. We must show Mowgli to the pack.'

The Law of the Jungle says that the pack must see all of the wolf cubs when they can walk, and look at them carefully.

1. **fight** : when people or animals fight, they use physical force to hurt each other.

UNDERSTANDING THE TEXT

1 COMPREHENSION CHECK

Read these sentences about Chapter One. Choose the correct answer (A, B or C).

1 Father and Mother Wolf hear a lot of noise coming from
   A ☐ a baby.
   B ☐ a cub.
   C ☐ a tiger.

2 The animals mustn't kill a man because
   A ☐ many men will come and kill the animals.
   B ☐ the Law of the Jungle says men are strong.
   C ☐ only Shere Kahn can kill men.

3 The baby starts to
   A ☐ cry.
   B ☐ look for food from its mother.
   C ☐ walk to its father.

4 Shere Kahn wants the 'cub' for himself because he wants to
   A ☐ eat it.
   B ☐ give it to the wolf pack.
   C ☐ take it back to the village.

5 The Law of the Jungle says that wolf cubs must
   A ☐ learn to walk immediately.
   B ☐ walk in front of the pack.
   C ☐ not talk to Shere Kahn.

6 'Mowgli' means
   A ☐ the monkey.
   B ☐ the frog.
   C ☐ the wolf cub.

'THE MAN CUB IS MINE'

We use **possessive pronouns** when we don't want to repeat a noun.

These are the possessive pronouns: mine   ours
                                     yours   yours
                                     his/hers   theirs

*Is that your cub? Yes, It's **ours**.*   **NOT**: *Yes, it's our cub.*
*I've got my umbrella. Have you got **yours**?*   **NOT**: *Have you got your umbrella?*
*I like my new clothes. I don't like **hers**.*   **NOT**: *I don't like her new clothes.*

12

2 POSSESSIVE PRONOUNS

Look at this picture of the jackal family. Read who the objects in the picture belong to. Write one sentence using a possessive pronoun. There is an example at the beginning (0).

0 The meat belongs to father jackal.   It is his.
1 The scarf belongs to mother jackal.   ....
2 The bone belongs to boy jackal.   ....
3 The pineapple belongs to girl jackal.   ....
4 The toy belongs to both the jackal children. ....

3 VOCABULARY
Put the words in the columns under the pictures.

legs   paws   nose   arms   ears   toes   tail   eyes

Words you can use about wolf cubs	Words you can use about both	Words you can use about babies
....	....	....
....	....	....
....	....	....
....	....	....
....	....	....
....	....	....

T: GRADE 2

4 SPEAKING: FAMILY AND FRIENDS
Mowgli becomes part of the wolf family and the cubs become his brothers and sisters. Talk to another student about your family and answer the questions.

1. Have you got any brothers or sisters? Describe them.
2. Have you got any pets? If so describe it/them.
3. How many friends have you got?
4. Tell the class about your favourite friend.
5. How often do you spend time together?
6. Does he/she live near your house?

BEFORE YOU READ

1 VOCABULARY

What are these things? Which of these things does a bear eat? What do monkeys eat?

1 ....

2 ....

3 ....

2 LISTENING

track 03

In Chapter Two you will read about a bear called Baloo and a panther called Bagheera. Listen to the information and complete the gaps.

My name (**1**) .... Baloo. I'm a big (**2**) .... I live (**3**) .... the jungle with Bagheera and the wolves. I (**4**) .... the cubs in the wolf pack about the Law (**5**) .... the Jungle. I know all the animals in the (**6**) .... I am their friend and (**7**) .... can speak their language. They know I don't hunt. I only (**8**) .... nuts and honey.

I'm Bagheera. I'm (**1**) .... black panther. (**2**) .... very strong. All the other animals say I'm clever. They often ask me about things (**3**) .... ask me to help them. I'm going (**4**) .... help Baloo teach Mowgli, the (**5**) .... cub. I know about men and I know they (**6**) .... clever, too. I hope (**7**) .... can teach him everything he needs to know to (**8**) .... in the jungle. It's a difficult place to live!

15

CHAPTER TWO
Council Rock[1]

When the four wolf cubs can walk, Father Wolf takes them and Mowgli to Council Rock. Mother Wolf goes too. Hundreds of wolves in the Wolf Pack meet at Council Rock once a month when the moon is full.

Akela is the leader of the Pack and he sits on a big rock. He is a grey wolf and he is very brave. Each new wolf cub stands in front of him and he says, 'Look carefully, wolves! Look carefully!'

At last Father Wolf pushes Mowgli in front of Akela and the other wolves.

'This is Mowgli the frog,' says Father Wolf. Mowgli just laughs.

Suddenly the wolves hear Shere Khan's voice behind the trees.

'The man cub is mine. Give him to me!' he cries.

Akela does not move, but says, 'Look carefully! Who speaks for this man cub? Two voices must speak for him, but not his father and mother.'

A big, sleepy brown bear appears in front of Akela.

'Baloo!' says Akela, surprised. Baloo teaches the Law of the Jungle to the wolf cubs and he speaks at the meetings of the

1. **Council Rock** : a place where the animals meet.

THE JUNGLE BOOK

Council. Everyone likes him because he eats only nuts and honey – he doesn't hunt.

'I can speak for the man cub,' says Baloo with his low voice. 'I can teach him to run with the Pack.'

'Very well,' says Akela.

Another animal silently jumps down into the circle of wolves. It is Bagheera the panther. He is black, brave and strong. He is also very clever.

'Akela, can I speak?' asks Bagheera softly.

'Yes, you can,' says Akela.

'The Law of the Jungle says it's possible to buy the life of a cub,' says Bagheera. 'It's bad to kill a man cub because he can't hurt you. Let him live and I can give you a fat bull to eat.'

'Good! Good!' say the young wolves. They are always hungry and want to eat the fat bull. 'Let him live!'

'Very well,' says Akela. 'Look carefully, wolves! Look carefully!'

The wolves walk near Mowgli and look at him carefully. Then they go away and only Akela, Baloo, Bagheera and Mowgli's wolf family are at the Council. They can hear Shere Khan roaring in the night.

'Men and their cubs are clever,' says Akela. 'One day this man cub can help us. Now take him away and teach him everything he must know.'

Thanks to Baloo's good words and Bagheera's fat bull, Mowgli now belongs to the Seeonee [1] Wolf Pack. He grows up in the wolf family and he learns the songs of the birds and the sounds of the animals in the jungle. Baloo and Bagheera are very good teachers. He learns to climb trees, swim in the river and hunt for his food. He is a happy boy.

1. **Seeonee** : the Indian name of the wolf pack.

UNDERSTANDING THE TEXT

1 COMPREHENSION CHECK

Are these sentences 'Right' (A) or 'Wrong' (B)? If there is not enough information to answer 'Right' (A) or 'Wrong' (B), choose 'Doesn't say' (C). There is an example at the beginning (0).

0   The wolf pack use Council Rock for meetings.
    (A) Right   B Wrong   C Doesn't say
1   Akela is the leader because he is very old.
    A Right   B Wrong   C Doesn't say
2   Shere Khan wants Mowgli.
    A Right   B Wrong   C Doesn't say
3   Baloo is a black panther.
    A Right   B Wrong   C Doesn't say
4   Baloo is a clever hunter.
    A Right   B Wrong   C Doesn't say
5   Bagheera is going to kill a bull.
    A Right   B Wrong   C Doesn't say
6   Akela thinks the man cub can help them.
    A Right   B Wrong   C Doesn't say
7   Baloo and Bagheera are going to teach Mowgli.
    A Right   B Wrong   C Doesn't say
8   Mowgli prefers swimming to climbing trees.
    A Right   B Wrong   C Doesn't say

2 CONVERSATION

Complete the conversation. What does Shere Khan say to Akela? For questions 1-5 mark the correct letter A–H. There is an example at the beginning (0).

0   Akela: What do you want Shere Khan?   Shere Khan   .G.
1   Akela: You can't have the man cub.   Shere Khan   .....
2   Akela: He is ours. We will pay the price.   Shere Khan   .....
3   Akela: Bagheera is going to kill a bull.   Shere Khan   .....
4   Akela: Yes, it is. Now you must go.   Shere Khan   .....
5   Akela: You can only return when he is big.   Shere Khan   .....

A When I return he is mine.
B One day I'm going to return.
C I don't want it.
D What are you going to give me?
E Why not?
F He isn't there.
G I want the man cub.
H Is this your price?

'YOU MUST GIVE IT TO ME!'

We use **must** when something is important or necessary.
Example: *Mowgli **must** learn the Law of the Jungle.*
We sometimes use **you + must** to tell someone to do something.
*You **must** leave Council Rock!*
We use **must not/mustn't** when we want to tell another person, very strongly, **not** to do something.
Example: *You **must not/mustn't** go away from the wolves' cave.*

3 MUST

Use *must* with a verb in the box to complete the Jungle Laws.

hunt   listen to   play   kill   stay   hurt

The Law of the Jungle

1 Animals .... not .... men. It is dangerous for all the animals to break this law.

2 Young animals .... with their mother until they are big.

3 Animals .... not .... an animal that knows the Master Words. He or she is part of our family.

4 Every animal .... in his or her own area and only take what he or she needs for food.

5 Animals that follow the Jungle Law .... not .... with the monkeys in the trees.

6 All animals .... their leader and follow the Jungle Law.

4 FILL IN THE GAPS

Read the information about wolves. Choose the correct answer (A, B or C) for each space (1-7).

Wolves are from the same family as dogs. They (**0**) ...A..... usually grey-brown in colour and they have blue or yellow eyes.

There are (**1**) .... wolves in North America and Northern Europe but it is possible to find wolves in hotter countries like Mexico and India too. Wolves often (**2**) .... in the forest, but in cold areas they live on icy open land called the Tundra. (**3**) .... eat large animals, such as bulls, and small animals too. If they are (**4**) ...., they eat the food that humans leave behind.

Wolves can live from 10 to 20 years. They live in a group of ten or more wolves, called a 'pack'. The pack (**5**) .... everything together. They travel, hunt and look after the cubs together. A strong, clever wolf (**6**) .... become the leader of the pack. This is not always a male wolf; (**7**) .... the leader is a female wolf.

Wolves have their cubs in the winter. The cubs leave the cave after nine weeks and they soon learn to do everything with the rest of the pack.

0	Ⓐ are	B is	C be
1	A much	B a lot of	C lot
2	A living	B live	C life
3	A Their	B They	C Them
4	A happy	B angry	C hungry
5	A has	B makes	C does
6	A can	B must	C is
7	A always	B never	C sometimes

BEFORE YOU READ

1 READING PICTURES

Look at the pictures in Chapter Three and answer the questions for both pictures.

1 Who can you see?
2 What are they doing?

CHAPTER **THREE**

Lessons with Baloo

Mowgli is now around ten years old. Baloo and Bagheera love him and they are good teachers. Baloo likes teaching Mowgli because he is a good student and learns quickly.

First he teaches him to hunt only when he is hungry and not for fun. Then he teaches him to speak to the different Jungle People and he teaches him the important Master Words.[1] Sometimes Mowgli gets tired of these lessons. One day he is not listening to his lesson and Baloo gets angry. He hits Mowgli gently on the head and the little boy runs away and climbs a tree.

'Baloo, don't hit little Mowgli!' says Bagheera. 'He's young! How can his little head remember all those long words?'

'Those long words keep him safe from all the birds, snakes and other animals in the jungle,' says Baloo. 'I know he's young but

---

1. **Master Words** : with these words Mowgli can talk to all the animals in the jungle.

the jungle is big and not always safe. There are dangers everywhere.' Then he turns around and calls Mowgli.

'Mowgli, come and say the Master Words again!'

Mowgli climbs down the tree and goes to sit with Baloo and Bagheera.

'I'm going to say the words to Bagheera, not to you, old Baloo!' says Mowgli. 'I know all the words!'

'Alright,' says Baloo. 'Say the words for the Hunting People.'

'We are of one blood, you and I,' says Mowgli.

'Good! Now say the words for the birds,' says Baloo.

THE JUNGLE BOOK

Mowgli says the same words but with the sound of a bird.

'And now for the Snake People,' says Baloo.

Mowgli says the same words but with the long 'sssss' sound of a snake.

'Very good!' says Baloo happily. 'With these words you are safe in the jungle, because no bird, snake or animal can hurt you.'

'Now I want to go up in the trees with my people,' says Mowgli happily.

'*What!*' says Baloo. 'Do you know the Monkey People?'

Suddenly Baloo and Bagheera are angry.

'Yes, I know the Monkey People,' says Mowgli. 'They take me up in the trees and give me good things to eat. They're kind to me and call me "brother". They play all day and don't do lessons. I like playing with them!'

'Oh, no!' says Baloo angrily. 'You know the law for all of the Jungle People, but the Monkey People don't have a law. They don't have a leader. They're dirty and noisy. They talk all day and forget everything they say. The Jungle People don't drink where the monkeys drink. We don't talk to them or think about them!'

'Forget the Monkey People, Mowgli,' says Bagheera. 'They live in the trees and they throw nuts [1] on our heads.'

'Oh...,' says Mowgli sadly. 'I'm very sorry.'

All this time the Monkey People are sitting in the trees and they are listening to Baloo, Bagheera and Mowgli. Suddenly they throw a lot of nuts and sticks on their heads. Baloo and Bagheera take Mowgli away to another part of the jungle and they take a nap. [2]

1. **nuts** :

2. **nap** : a short sleep during the day.

UNDERSTANDING THE TEXT

1 QUESTIONS
Put the words in the correct order to make questions. Ask another student the questions and answer them.

1. Mowgli/is/How/old? ....
2. does/him/hit/Why/Baloo? ....
3. Master Words/What/the/are? ....
4. jungle/Why/Mowgli/the/in/safe/is? ....
5. Mowgli/do/does/to/What/want? ....
6. to/is/them/listening/Who? ....

KET

2 CONVERSATIONS
Complete the five conversations. For questions 1-5 mark A, B or C.

1. Do you know all the words?
   - A ☐ Yes, I do.
   - B ☐ No, they aren't.
   - C ☐ I can't.

2. How do you say 'one blood' in bird language?
   - A ☐ I don't know.
   - B ☐ Yes, it is.
   - C ☐ Nothing.

3. Where is Bagheera?
   - A ☐ Yes, he's here.
   - B ☐ Under the tree.
   - C ☐ A panther.

4. Do you like school?
   - A ☐ I hate.
   - B ☐ No, it's not.
   - C ☐ I prefer to play.

5. Can I play with the monkeys?
   - A ☐ Not.
   - B ☐ No, you can't.
   - C ☐ They can't.

'I'M GOING TO SAY THE WORDS TO BAGHEERA'

We use **going to** when we have a definite plan to do something in the future. We use the verb **to be** + **going to** + verb (e.g. *watch*).

Example: *We're going to spend our holidays at the sea this summer.*

3 LISTENING

Listen to Baloo talking to Mowgli about the things they are going to do today. Complete the sentences with what they are going to do. There is an example at the beginning (0).

0   In the morning ..they are going to find.... some nuts for breakfast.
1   Mowgli .... all the Master Words.
2   Baloo and Mowgli .... some bananas from the trees.
3   Baloo .... some honey for them to eat.
4   Bagheera .... his own lunch.
5   After lunch Baloo and Bagheera ....
6   Then Mowgli .... with Bagheera.

4 FILL IN THE GAPS

Complete this letter. Write one word for each space. There is an example at the beginning (0).

> Hi!
> My name (0) ....is............ Rohan. I live (1) .... a small village in India, near Madras. I go (2) .... school in the same village. My brother (3) .... to the Chennai II High School in Madras. He travels there by bus.
>
> I like (4) .... school very much. We study a lot of different subjects. We (5) .... English and Maths in the morning and Science, History (6) .... Geography in the afternoon. Sometimes we (7) .... cricket outside. Cricket (8) .... my favourite sport.
> Tell me about your school.
> Your friend
> Rohan

5 WRITING

Write a note (25-35 words) to your friend about your school. Say:

- where your school is and how you get there.
- what your favourite subjects are.
- what sports you do at school.

6 VOCABULARY
Do you know the names of these objects? Use a dictionary if necessary.

T: GRADE 2

7 SPEAKING: YOUR CLASSROOM
Ask and answer questions about your classroom and classroom objects with another student.

- what have you got in your pencil case?
- how many students are there in your class?
- what can you see on the wall?

BEFORE YOU READ

1 LISTENING
Listen to Chapter Four. Tick T (true) or F (false).

track 07

		T	F
1	Mowgli is in the trees with the monkeys.	☐	☐
2	Mowgli speaks to a bird.	☐	☐
3	Rann does not understand him.	☐	☐
4	A snake tells Baloo and Bagheera about Mowgli.	☐	☐
5	Bagheera says that they are looking for food.	☐	☐
6	The snake is angry with the monkeys.	☐	☐

CHAPTER **FOUR**

Kaa

When Baloo and Bagheera wake up after their nap, they can't find Mowgli.

'Where's Mowgli?' asks Bagheera.

Baloo looks up at a tree and sees Mowgli. The Monkey People are holding his legs and arms! Baloo shouts angrily and Bagheera tries to climb up the tree. But he is too heavy for the small branches. [1] The monkeys laugh loudly and carry Mowgli away.

Baloo and Bagheera are very angry and worried. They follow the monkeys and Mowgli, but the monkeys move very quickly.

It is exciting for Mowgli to fly in the sky. The monkeys jump quickly from tree to tree, but Mowgli is afraid of falling.

'Where are the monkeys taking me?' he thinks. 'I must tell Baloo and Bagheera. But how?'

Suddenly he sees Rann. He is a big bird and he flies high in

1. branches :

THE JUNGLE BOOK

the blue sky. Rann sees the monkeys with a man cub. He flies down and hears the Master Words of the birds. 'We are of one blood, you and I!'

'You speak our language,' says Rann. 'Who are you?'

'I'm Mowgli the man cub. Please help me! Find Baloo and Bagheera and tell them about the monkeys.'

'Alright!' says Rann. 'I can do that!' And he flies away.

The monkeys move quickly and soon Baloo and Bagheera are far behind.

'We're too slow,' says Baloo. 'We can't follow the monkeys. Poor Mowgli, he is in danger!'

'Poor Mowgli!' says Bagheera. 'Oh, this is terrible!' His big green eyes are sad. 'I have an idea! Where's Kaa, the giant python?[1] He climbs up trees quickly and easily, and he eats monkeys! Perhaps he can help us.'

'A clever idea, Bagheera!' says Baloo. 'Let's look for him.'

They find Kaa lying in the sun. He is a beautiful yellow and brown snake, and he is ten metres long. He is very strong and very dangerous.

'Hello!' says Kaa when he sees them.

'Hello, Kaa!' says Baloo. 'We're looking for food.'

'Oh, I'm very hungry,' says Kaa. 'Let me come with you.'

'We're following the Monkey People,' says Baloo. 'They have our man cub and we want to find him.'

'Why are you following the Monkey People?' asks Kaa.

'They took our man cub and we're angry,' says Baloo.

'We must find him now,' says Bagheera.

1. **python** :

THE JUNGLE BOOK

Kaa looks interested and says, 'Your man cub?'

'Yes,' says Baloo. 'Our man cub, Mowgli.'

Bagheera is very clever and says, 'The Monkey People always call you bad names. They say you're an old, yellow worm.'[1]

'Sssss!' says Kaa angrily. 'Those noisy, dirty monkeys must not call me bad names! Where are they? And where is your man cub?'

Suddenly they hear a voice from the sky.

'Look up, Baloo!' shouts Rann.

'Hello, Rann!' shouts Baloo.

'Mowgli's with the Monkey People,' cries Rann. 'He's in the monkey city – the Lost City! Mowgli's clever, he knows the Master Words. Good luck!'

'The Lost City!' says Bagheera, surprised. 'It's a very old city and no one lives there.'

'Yes,' says Baloo, 'only the Monkey People go there. We must leave immediately because it's far away. You move quickly, but I'm slow. I can follow you.'

'Yes, let's go!' says Kaa. 'I'm very hungry. Those noisy monkeys can't call me an old, yellow worm! I'm going to teach them something!'

1. worm :

UNDERSTANDING THE TEXT

1 COMPREHENSION CHECK

Read this summary of Chapter Four. Choose the correct answer (A, B or C) for each space. There is an example at the beginning (0).

Baloo and Bagheera (**0**) ..*are*........ sleeping. When they wake up, they (**1**) .... find Mowgli. They see that the monkeys have Mowgli. Baloo (**2**) .... Bagheera try to follow Mowgli and the monkeys (**3**) .... the monkeys are moving too quickly.

Mowgli sees a bird (**4**) .... Rann. He speaks to him (**5**) .... the birds' language. 'Go and tell Baloo and Bagheera about me,' he says.

Baloo and Bagheera (**6**) .... to the snake, Kaa. 'Mowgli is with the monkeys. The monkeys (**7**) .... call you bad names. Come (**8**) .... us to find him.'

Rann (**9**) .... and he tells Baloo and Bagheera that the monkeys are (**10**) .... Mowgli to the Lost City.

Baloo, Bagheera and Kaa go to find Mowgli. Kaa is very (**11**) .... that the monkeys call him (**12**) .... names.

0	Ⓐ are	B is	C aren't
1	A cannot	B mustn't	C haven't
2	A also	B with	C and
3	A but	B not	C and
4	A is	B name	C called
5	A in	B by	C at
6	A speak	B look	C watch
7	A usual	B never	C always
8	A with	B next	C together
9	A sees	B return	C arrives
10	A bring	B taking	C have
11	A happily	B comfortable	C angry
12	A bad	B exciting	C boring

'WE'RE FOLLOWING THE MONKEY PEOPLE'

We use the **present continuous** to describe something that is happening at the moment we speak. To form the **present continuous** we use **to be + a verb + 'ing'**.

Example: *Look! The monkeys **are taking** Mowgli to the Lost City!*

2 PRESENT CONTINUOUS

Look at the pictures and describe them using the present continuous. There is an example at the beginning (0).

0 The bird is flying.

3 VOCABULARY – ANIMALS

Look at the descriptions of eight animals (1-8). Match them to an animal (A-H).

A lion B crocodile C zebra D giraffe
E hippopotamus F elephant G orangutan H frog

1 ☐ I have black and white stripes. I'm similar to a horse and I can run fast.
2 ☐ I'm yellow with black spots. I have a long neck so I can eat leaves from high trees.
3 ☐ I'm small and green. I have big eyes and long back legs. I like swimming and I can jump high.
4 ☐ I'm long and green. I have big teeth and I can swim underwater.
5 ☐ I'm big and grey. I can carry heavy things and people on my back.
6 ☐ I'm big and fat. I can stay underwater for a long time.
7 ☐ I have orange fur and long arms and legs. I can jump from one tree to another.
8 ☐ I have yellow fur. I am brave and strong and I can run fast.

4 LISTENING

Listen to the animals. What can they do? Write the letter of the animal next to a verb. You can use the animals more than once.

A Rann   **B** Bagheera   **C** Kaa   **D** Shere Khan   **E** Baloo

1. ☐ fly
2. ☐ jump
3. ☐ dance
4. ☐ speak other languages
5. ☐ swim
6. ☐ run
7. ☐ sing
8. ☐ hunt

What can Mowgli do? What can you do?

5 WORD GAME

Find the animals in the word square.

lion   crocodile   zebra   giraffe   hippopotamus
elephant   orangutan   frog

```
S F G H S G F A N E Z
W U P I S A F L A V L E
C V M H R L X T Q J I B
W C A A S A U R M U D R
G O R F T G F W Z H O A
Q U Y M N O X F S P C Q
F P U A U V P S E M O Q
A O R F Y N R O A L R S
E O P N M U V W P L C Q
E L E P H A N T I P B B
J X H F W G S O G Y I Q
V K K M T K N I K F L H
```

6 A JUNGLE MESSAGE

Read this jungle message from the birds. Look at the key below for the missing letters.

H◉lp! ▼■loo ■n● ▼■✲h◉◉r■ must ✧in● Mow✲li. Pl◉■s◉ ✧ly to ☆ouncil Ro☆k ■n● t◉ll the wolv◉s th◉ monk◉ys ■r◉ t■kin✲ Mow✲li to th◉ Lost ☆ity. Th◉y ■r◉ ▼■● ■nd th◉y ●o not ✧ollow our l■ws.

CLUES: c ☆   b ▼   g ✲   d ●   f ✧   e ◉   a ■

CHAPTER **FIVE**

The Lost City

Everything in the Lost City is very old. There is a big palace on a hill and a water fountain near the king's garden. The houses don't have any roofs¹ and trees are growing inside them.

The Monkey People call this place *their* city and run around everywhere.

Some monkeys play with the oranges and flowers in the king's garden, and then they fight and shout. Others jump up and down and say silly² things.

The Monkey People are happy because Mowgli is with them.

'This boy can teach us how to make things,' says one monkey.

'Yes, men make things with their hands,' says another monkey.

1. **roofs** :

2. **silly** : stupid.

THE JUNGLE BOOK

But monkeys always forget the things they say.

Mowgli is tired and hungry, and says, 'Bring me some food.' About thirty noisy monkeys go to get some fruit. But they start fighting and forget to bring the fruit to Mowgli.

Mowgli doesn't like the monkeys or the Lost City. 'Baloo's right,' he thinks, 'the Monkey People have no law. They are different from us. I must try to run away. Baloo and Bagheera are probably angry with me!'

Mowgli tries to run to the walls of the Lost City, but the monkeys pull him back.

'You mustn't go away,' they shout. 'You're happy here with us. We're great. We're wonderful! We all say this and it's true!'

Mowgli is tired and confused. 'When do these monkeys sleep?' he thinks. He looks up at the sky and sees a big cloud near the moon. 'Perhaps that cloud is going to hide the moon, and I can run away when it's dark.'

Bagheera and Kaa are also watching the same cloud. They are outside the walls of the Lost City.

'We must be careful,' says Bagheera. 'There are only two of us and there are hundreds of monkeys. They are near the walls and they're talking to Mowgli. When the cloud hides the moon I'm going to attack them.'

'Good idea!' says Kaa. 'I'm going to go up the hill and then I'm going to come down fast.'

Bagheera enters the city walls silently and attacks the monkeys. He hits them with his strong, black paws. The monkeys are scared and scream. But one of them shouts, 'Bagheera is alone! Kill him! Kill him!'

THE JUNGLE BOOK

Suddenly hundreds of monkeys jump on Bagheera and hit, kick and bite [1] him. Bagheera fights bravely but he is alone.

Other monkeys take Mowgli to an old, broken building. They throw him into a dark room with one small window. 'Stay here with the Poison [2] People until we kill your friend Bagheera,' says one monkey. 'Then we can play.'

In the dark room Mowgli can hear the hissing sounds of the Poison People.

'This room is full of snakes!' he thinks. 'I must give the Snakes' Call.'

'We are all one blood, you and I,' he says, giving the Snakes' Call.

'Sssssss,' the snakes answer. 'We're not going to bite you, but please don't move because your feet hurt us.'

'Alright!' says Mowgli, listening to the noise of the fight outside.

'Bagheera's fighting for his life!' thinks Mowgli. 'How can I help him?'

He remembers the big water fountain near the king's garden.

He goes to the small window and shouts, 'Bagheera! Go to the water fountain and jump into the water!'

Bagheera hears him and thinks, 'Oh, good, Mowgli is safe!' He slowly goes to the water fountain.

Finally Baloo arrives and shouts, 'Bagheera, I'm here!'

The monkeys jump on Baloo and he hits them with his big, strong arms. Mowgli hears a loud splash when Bagheera jumps into the water fountain. The monkeys are afraid of water and they stand around the fountain. Bagheera cannot get out to help Baloo.

1. **bite** : you do this with your teeth.
2. **Poison** : something that can make you ill or kill you.

UNDERSTANDING THE TEXT

1 COMPREHENSION CHECK

Read these sentences about Chapter Five. Choose the correct answer (A, B or C).

1 The monkeys are happy that Mowgli is with them because
   A ☐ he can play with them.
   B ☐ he speaks their language.
   C ☐ he can teach them things.

2 The monkeys don't bring Mowgli any food because
   A ☐ they always forget things.
   B ☐ they want to play.
   C ☐ there is no fruit.

3 Mowgli is watching the cloud because
   A ☐ he thinks he can escape when it is dark.
   B ☐ he knows Baloo and Bagheera are watching it too.
   C ☐ the monkeys go to sleep when it is dark.

4 The monkeys jump on Bagheera because
   A ☐ he is not strong.
   B ☐ he is alone.
   C ☐ he hits them.

5 The snakes say to Mowgli:
   A ☐ 'Go away!'
   B ☐ 'We are going to bite you!'
   C ☐ 'You are hurting us!'

6 The monkeys are afraid of
   A ☐ Baloo.
   B ☐ the water of the fountain.
   C ☐ the snakes.

2 CHARACTERS

Put the letters in the correct order to make adjectives. Match the adjectives (1-6) to the characters below (A-E). There can be more than one adjective for each character.

A Baloo   B Bagheera   C Mowgli   D Kaa   E the monkeys

1 ☐ gdenruaso
2 ☐ nurgyh
3 ☐ idnk
4 ☐ rgtosn
5 ☐ cverle
6 ☐ iylsl

3 VOCABULARY

Read these definitions of places. What is the word for each one? The first letter is already there. There is one space for each other letter of the word. There is an example at the beginning (0).

0 a long area of water that goes from the land to the sea   r i v e r
1 high land, smaller than a mountain   h _ _ _
2 a large area of hard stone   r _ _ _
3 an area of many trees close together   f _ _ _ _ _
4 a tropical area of trees and plants   j _ _ _ _ _
5 sand or rocks near the sea   b _ _ _ _
6 a large town   c _ _ _

4 LISTENING

You will hear someone asking for some information about a trip to the Lost City of Azkan. Listen and complete the missing information.

Jungle Adventure Tour to (**1**) .... of Azkan.
Date of next trip (**2**) ....
Tour leaves at (**3**) ....
Place to meet (**4**) ....
Name on reservation (**5**) ....
Price per person (**6**) ....

45

Let's meet some of the animals in the story!

🔊 Tigers

There are five kinds of tigers in the world: the Siberian, the Bengal, the Indochinese, the South Chinese and the Sumatran.

Tigers are big, strong animals and they live in Asia. They are carnivorous and they hunt alone at night, because they have excellent night vision. They are also good swimmers.

There are only about 7,000 tigers in the world today. They are in danger of extinction [1] and this is very sad. People hunt them for their beautiful coats [2] and this is against the law. Many countries are trying to save tigers.

1. **extinction** : when a kind of animal doesn't exist anymore.
2. **coat** : the fur of the animal.

Bears

There are different kinds of bears in the world: the black bear, the grizzly, the kodiak, the Alaskan brown bear and the polar bear.

Bears are very big and heavy, and have a lot of fur. They are strong, lively animals. They live in the forests and mountains of North America, Asia and Europe – but polar bears live in the Arctic Circle. They are carnivorous animals but they also like fish, fruit and honey.

Indian Pythons

Indian pythons are from the family of snakes. They are very big, long snakes and live in the jungles of India. They like living near water.

They kill animals by squeezing [1] them. They don't chew their food – they swallow their prey! Indian pythons can even eat big animals like deer. [2] After a big meal they don't eat for days or weeks.

Pythons are in danger of extinction too. People hunt them for their beautiful skin, and use it to make bags, shoes and belts. In some countries this is against the law.

1. **squeezing** :  2. **deer** :

Black Panthers

Black panthers are really black leopards. Their coat is very dark so you cannot see its spots. Black panthers live in Asia, Africa and the Far East. They are carnivorous and they live in forests and jungles. They like climbing up trees and sitting there. They are strong, clever animals and they hunt at night.

Wolves

Wolves are social animals. They live and hunt together in a pack. Each pack has a leader and the other wolves must follow him.

There are grey, brown, black, red and white wolves. They communicate with different sounds – they howl, bark and growl.

Wolves live in the forests and mountains of Alaska, the United States, Northern Europe and Russia. They are in danger of extinction too! There are only about 150,000 wolves in the world today. Many of them live in national parks in the United States. Many countries have laws that protect wolves.

1 COMPREHENSION CHECK
Are these sentences true (T) or false (F)? Correct the false ones.

		T	F
1	Tigers live in Asia and Africa.	☐	☐
2	They eat meat and hunt at night.	☐	☐
3	Today there are about 7,000 tigers in the world.	☐	☐
4	The grizzly and the kodiak are bears.	☐	☐
5	Polar bears live in the Arctic Circle.	☐	☐
6	The Indian python lives in the mountains of India.	☐	☐
7	It can only eat small animals.	☐	☐
8	The black panther eats only fruit and honey.	☐	☐
9	Wolves live together in a pack.	☐	☐
10	They are not in danger of extinction.	☐	☐
11	People hunt animals for their beautiful coats and skins.	☐	☐
12	Many countries have laws that protect animals.	☐	☐

BEFORE YOU READ

KET

1 LISTENING

track 12

Listen to the first part of Chapter Six and choose the correct answer (A, B or C).

1 The monkeys are afraid of Kaa because
   A ☐ he can kill any animal.
   B ☐ he is very big.
   C ☐ he is unfriendly.

2 Kaa hits the wall with his body three times and
   A ☐ goes away.
   B ☐ hurts his head.
   C ☐ makes a hole in it.

3 Kaa moves in front of the monkeys and
   A ☐ talks to them.
   B ☐ begins the Hunger Dance.
   C ☐ starts eating.

4 The monkeys are terrified and
   A ☐ they start crying.
   B ☐ they run away.
   C ☐ they are suddenly quiet.

CHAPTER SIX

Kaa's Dance

Suddenly Kaa comes down the hill fast and he is ready to attack the monkeys. They all know that Kaa can kill any animal and they are afraid of him. When they see him, they shout, 'It's Kaa! Run! Run!'

Then Kaa opens his mouth and speaks one hissing word. The monkeys are suddenly quiet and everything in the Lost City is silent.

Bagheera gets out of the fountain. 'Let's take Mowgli and go!' he says. 'Thank you, Kaa.'

'Yes, thank you, Kaa,' says Baloo. 'You're great. Look at the monkeys! They're terrified!' [1]

'I'm happy to help,' says Kaa. 'Where's the man cub?'

'I'm here with the snakes!' cries Mowgli. 'I can't get out!'

'Take him away,' shout the snakes. 'He jumps around and hurts us with his feet.'

'Ha! The man cub has friends everywhere,' says Kaa. He hits the wall with his heavy body three times and makes a hole [2] in it. Mowgli jumps out and runs to Baloo and Bagheera.

'Thank you for helping me,' says Mowgli, smiling.

1. **terrified** : very scared, very afraid.

2. **hole** :

'You must thank Kaa,' say Baloo and Bagheera.

Mowgli looks at the great python.

'He looks a bit like a monkey,' says Kaa.

'We're of one blood, you and I,' says Mowgli. 'I'm your friend and I can always help you.'

'You're brave and you speak well,' says Kaa. 'Now you must go with your friends.'

Kaa moves softly in front of the sitting monkeys and begins his dance – the Hunger [1] Dance. His head moves slowly from right to left. His long body makes circles, squares and other shapes. He dances slowly and never stops. The monkeys are terrified but they cannot move.

1. **Hunger** : the feeling you get when you are hungry.

THE JUNGLE BOOK

Baloo and Bagheera look at Kaa and cannot move. Mowgli cannot understand what is happening.

'Monkeys!' cries Kaa. 'Can you move?'

'No, Kaa,' they answer loudly, 'without your word we cannot move.'

'Come close to me, monkeys,' says Kaa in his low voice. 'Come very close!'

The monkeys move close to Kaa, and Baloo and Bagheera move close too. Mowgli is worried and he pulls Baloo and Bagheera away.

'Oh, thank you, Mowgli,' whispers [1] Bagheera.

'What's happening?' asks Mowgli. 'Your eyes are closing! Are you feeling well?'

'A python's dance is magic,' whispers Bagheera. 'It's very dangerous to watch even for us, because it's easy to walk into his mouth!'

'Oh!' says Mowgli, surprised.

The monkeys are moving close to Kaa.

'Kaa is going to have a big dinner tonight with all of those monkeys!' whispers Baloo. 'Let's go back to the jungle, quickly.'

Baloo, Bagheera and Mowgli leave the Lost City. They go back to the jungle.

'And now, Mowgli,' says Bagheera, 'we must follow the Law of the Jungle – we must punish [2] you for talking to the monkeys.'

'You're right,' says Mowgli, 'I'm a bad man cub.' He looks at Baloo sadly.

'We're sorry, but we cannot go against the Law of the Jungle,' says Baloo.

---

1. **whispers** : speaks very quietly.
2. **punish** : to make someone suffer because he/she does something wrong.

Kaa's Dance

'You must learn, Mowgli,' says Bagheera.

Bagheera hits him softly with his big paw six times, but Mowgli does not cry.

'You're a brave man cub,' says Baloo.

'Now,' Bagheera says, 'jump on my back, Little Brother, and always remember to follow the Law of the Jungle. It's a good law and it keeps you safe. Let's go home!'

'Yes,' says Mowgli. 'I want to go home.' He soon falls asleep on Bagheera's back.

UNDERSTANDING THE TEXT

1 COMPREHENSION CHECK

Are these sentences 'Right' (A) or 'Wrong' (B)? If there is not enough information to answer 'Right' (A) or 'Wrong' (B), choose 'Doesn't say' (C). There is an example at the beginning (0).

0   The monkeys are afraid of Kaa.
    (A) Right   B Wrong   C Doesn't say
1   Kaa does not like the other snakes.
    A Right   B Wrong   C Doesn't say
2   Kaa helps Mowgli to escape.
    A Right   B Wrong   C Doesn't say
3   Baloo says that Mowgli looks like a monkey.
    A Right   B Wrong   C Doesn't say
4   Mowgli falls asleep when Kaa does his dance.
    A Right   B Wrong   C Doesn't say
5   Kaa is going to have dinner when the moon is full.
    A Right   B Wrong   C Doesn't say
6   Bagheera punishes Mowgli.
    A Right   B Wrong   C Doesn't say

2 COMPREHENSION CHECK

Choose the correct answer (A or B).

1   Why does Kaa think Mowgli is a monkey?
    A ☐ Men and monkeys are from the same family.
    B ☐ Mowgli likes to play with the monkeys.

2   'Kaa is going to have a big dinner tonight with all those monkeys.' What does this mean?
    A ☐ He and the monkeys are going to have dinner.
    B ☐ He is going to eat them.

3   What is Kaa's dance?
    A ☐ The dance a snake makes to catch other animals.
    B ☐ A dance to make other animals fall asleep so he can escape.

4   Why do Baloo and Bagheera almost fall asleep?
    A ☐ Kaa's dance confuses them.
    B ☐ They are very tired because they are helping Mowgli.

3 PICTURE SUMMARY
Number these pictures from the story in the right order.

A B C D 1 E F

4 VOCABULARY
Look at the dinner table. What food can you see?

5 SPEAKING
Tell another student about the food you like to eat.

BEFORE YOU READ

1 VOCABULARY
Match the words in the box to the pictures.

hill   village   fire pot   fire   leaves
coat   cloth   stick   tears

2 READING PICTURES
Look at the picture on page 61 and answer these questions.

1 What can you see in the picture?
2 Is Mowgli talking to the other boy?
3 If so, what do you think they are talking about?
4 Where are they?
5 Is the animal eating?

CHAPTER **SEVEN**

The Red Flower

All of the Jungle People are Mowgli's friends, but not Shere Khan.

Bagheera tells Mowgli, 'Be careful of Shere Khan, he wants to kill you. Akela likes you, but he's old now. He's not strong. The young wolves don't listen to him. They listen to Shere Khan. One day you must kill him.'

'I'm not afraid!' says Mowgli laughing. 'I have you and Baloo.'

'Mowgli, you must listen to me,' says Bagheera softly. 'Remember, you're a man cub, not a wolf cub. You belong to the world of men. They're your brothers. One day you must return to that world. You're clever and you can do a lot of things we can't do, because you're a man.'

'Yes, Mowgli,' says Baloo, 'Shere Khan's making trouble for you. The young wolves want to kill you.'

'But why?' asks Mowgli.

'Look at me,' says Bagheera. Mowgli looks him in the eyes, but Bagheera turns his head away quickly.

'That's why,' he says. 'You see, Mowgli, even I can't look into your eyes. You're a man; you're clever. The young wolves know this and they hate you.'

THE JUNGLE BOOK

Mowgli listens to Bagheera and Baloo quietly.

'You must go to the men's village and take some of their Red Flower,' says Bagheera. 'All of the animals are afraid of it. It's a strong friend and it can help you.'

The Red Flower is fire, but the animals do not call it by its name.

'Very well,' says Mowgli. 'I'm going to the men's village to get the Red Flower now.'

In the village he sees a young boy cover a fire pot with a cloth. Mowgli takes the pot from the boy and runs back to the jungle.

That evening the jackal Tabaqui goes to see Mowgli and says, 'There's a meeting at Council Rock tomorrow morning.'

When Mowgli gets to Council Rock, Akela is not sitting on top of the big rock. He is sitting next to it. Shere Khan is there, too, and all of the young wolves are sitting around him. Mowgli sits next to Bagheera with the fire pot between his legs.

Shere Khan starts speaking and Mowgli jumps up.

'Is Shere Khan your leader?' asks Mowgli. 'Does he belong to the Wolf Pack?'

'Akela's old now, he's not important,' says Shere Khan. 'Listen to me! A man cub doesn't belong to a Wolf Pack. Give him to me!'

'A man!' cry the young wolves. 'A man doesn't belong to our Wolf Pack.'

Akela is angry and says, 'Mowgli's our brother. He respects the Law of the Jungle. Let him go away safely.'

'But he's a man!' cry Shere Khan and some of the wolves.

Mowgli is very angry. He stands up with the fire pot in his hands.

He takes a piece of wood and puts it in the fire. It starts

THE JUNGLE BOOK

burning. The wolves and the tiger are afraid of the fire and move away from Mowgli.

'You're the leader now,' says Bagheera. 'Help your friend Akela!'

'I want to go to my people,' says Mowgli, 'but first... .' He goes to Shere Khan and says, 'You want to kill me but now you're afraid of me!' He hits Shere Khan on the head with his burning stick and burns it a bit. The tiger is terrified.

'Go away now!' says Mowgli. 'But remember, I'm going to kill you one day. And you must not kill my friend Akela. He is free to live in the jungle.'

Mowgli jumps at the young wolves with his burning stick. They are terrified and run away with Shere Khan. Only Akela, Bagheera and some old wolves stay at Council Rock.

Suddenly something inside Mowgli hurts and he starts crying.

'What's happening to me?' he asks Bagheera. 'Am I dying?'

'You're a man and these are... tears,' says Bagheera. 'They're only tears. Now you must go to your people. You can't stay in the jungle any more, my Little Brother.'

'Yes, I must go to the world of men,' says Mowgli. 'But first I want to say goodbye to my mother and father.'

He goes to the cave and cries on his mother's coat.

'Please don't forget me!' says Mowgli, crying.

'Forget you?' says Mother Wolf. 'Never! We love you!'

'Come and visit us often,' says Father Wolf. 'Your mother and I are getting old.'

'When I come to visit, I'm going to bring Shere Khan's coat!' says Mowgli.

The next morning he goes down the hill to the world of men.

UNDERSTANDING THE TEXT

1 SUMMARY
Complete the sentences. Choose the correct ending (A-J) to make a summary of the story.

1 ☐ The young wolves want to kill Mowgli
2 ☐ Mowgli must go to the village
3 ☐ The Red Flower is the name
4 ☐ Mowgli returns with
5 ☐ At the meeting Shere Khan
6 ☐ Mowgli takes a piece of wood
7 ☐ Shere Khan and the wolves are scared of the fire
8 ☐ Mowgli starts to cry
9 ☐ Mowgli wants to stay with the wolves
10 ☐ He says he is going to kill

A to get the Red Flower.
B the fire in a fire pot.
C but he doesn't understand tears.
D but he must return to his people.
E and it starts burning.
F the animals give to 'fire'.
G Shere Khan and bring back his coat.
H is sitting on the rock.
I because he is a man.
J and they run away.

2 PLACES IN THE STORY
Match the sentences to the places in the story.

1 ☐ Mowgli lives here with the wolf cubs.
2 ☐ The wolves have their meetings here.
3 ☐ Mowgli does lessons here with Baloo and Bagheera.
4 ☐ The monkeys take Mowgli here.
5 ☐ Mowgli goes to live here when he is a man.

A the Lost City   B the village
C the cave   D in the jungle
E Council Rock

3 CHARACTERS

Who says this? Match a character (A-F) to the sentences they say (1-6).

A   Mowgli
B   Shere Khan
C   Baloo
D   Kaa
E   Bagheera
F   Akela

1   'The man cub is mine!'
2   'Who speaks for this man cub?'
3   'I want him to be safe in this big jungle.'
4   'Come close to me, monkeys.'
5   'I'm going to kill you one day.'
6   'Now you must go to your people.'

4 VOCABULARY – CLOTHES

Mowgli says he is going to bring back Shere Khan's coat. A 'coat' is another word for the fur animals have. It is also something people wear. Match a word to a picture for each of these clothes.

jumper   trainers   jacket   trousers   skirt   hat

1 ____   2 ____   3 ____
4 ____   5 ____   6 ____

T: GRADE 2

5 SPEAKING: CLOTHES
Answer the questions.

1. Describe the clothes you like to wear.
2. Describe the clothes of the student sitting next to you.
3. What is you teacher wearing?
4. Do you prefer buying shoes or clothes?
5. Do you buy clothes or shoes with friends?
6. What are your favourite colours?

6 QUIZ
Do the jungle quiz. Check your answers on page 80.

1. Which country does NOT have a jungle?
   - A ☐ Brazil
   - B ☐ India
   - C ☐ Canada

2. Which of these jungle cats lives in the Amazon?
   - A ☐ lion
   - B ☐ jaguar
   - C ☐ tiger

3. What do people in the jungle sometimes use plants for?
   - A ☐ to help people when they are ill
   - B ☐ to make expensive jewellery to sell
   - C ☐ to make paper to write on

4. What do monkeys like to eat?
   - A ☐ insects, fruit and flowers
   - B ☐ insects and meat
   - C ☐ fruit and rice

5. Which of these sentences about the jungle is true?
   - A ☐ There is a lot of sun.
   - B ☐ It rains a lot.
   - C ☐ There are not many insects.

CHAPTER **EIGHT**

Tiger! Tiger!

'I have a lot of enemies now,' Mowgli thinks. 'I must go far away.'

He runs and runs until he comes to a village near a lot of rocks and ravines.¹ He sees cows and buffaloes² everywhere. Some boys are looking after them. When they see Mowgli they run away.

'Men here are afraid of the People of the Jungle,' thinks Mowgli.

Mowgli sits near the village gate. When he sees a man he opens his mouth to show that he wants some food. The man is surprised and runs to the village shouting. He comes back with about a hundred people. Everyone looks at Mowgli.

'Look, he has the bite marks³ of wolves on his arms and legs!' says one man. 'He's a wolf child – he comes from the jungle!'

'These men don't understand,' thinks Mowgli. 'I don't have bite

1. **ravines** : narrow valleys with high walls of rock. See picture

2. **buffalo** :     3. **bite marks** :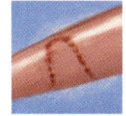

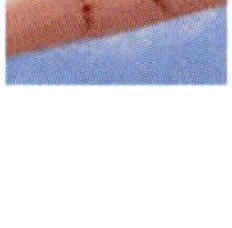

THE JUNGLE BOOK

marks – I have play marks. Wolf cubs always bite lightly when they play!'

'He's a good-looking boy,' says one woman, 'but he's thin.'

'He must eat, poor boy,' says Messua, another woman. 'He can come home with me.'

Messua takes Mowgli to her house and gives him some bread and milk. She is kind to him.

'This is my first time in a house and I don't like it,' thinks Mowgli. 'But I'm a man now and I must do what men do. I know the languages of the jungle and now I must learn the language of men.'

That day Mowgli learns a lot of words from Messua. But at night he does not want to sleep inside a house. He climbs out of a small window and goes to sleep under a big tree near the village. He meets Grey Brother, a wolf cub.

'Hello Little Brother,' says Grey Brother. 'I have news for you. Shere Khan's in the mountains now, but he wants to kill you when he comes back!'

'Please come to the big tree and tell me when Shere Khan comes back,' says Mowgli.

'Yes, Little Brother,' says Grey Brother. 'And don't forget your wolf family.'

'I can't forget the family I love!' says Mowgli, smiling.

For three months Mowgli lives in the village. He learns to wear clothes, use money and work. Every day he looks after cows and buffaloes.

One day Mowgli sees Grey Brother at the big tree.

'Shere Khan is back!' says Grey Brother. 'He wants to meet you outside the village gate tonight. But now he's hiding in the big ravine.'

THE JUNGLE BOOK

'Thank you, Grey Brother!' says Mowgli. He thinks for a moment. Then he looks at Grey Brother and says, 'The big ravine! I can take the buffaloes to the top and run after Shere Khan down the ravine. The cows can stay at the bottom of the ravine. In this way he's between the buffaloes and the cows and he can't run away!'

'You're right!' says Grey Brother excitedly.

'Can you help me?' asks Mowgli.

'Akela and I can help you!' says Grey Brother, and Akela comes out from the trees.

'Akela!' cries Mowgli happily. 'You're a true friend!'

'Take the cows to the bottom of the ravine, Grey Brother,' says Mowgli. 'Akela and I are going to take the buffaloes to the top.'

When Mowgli is ready he shouts, 'Shere Khan! It's me, Mowgli! Are you ready?' Mowgli gets on Rama, one of the buffaloes, and they all start running down the ravine.

Shere Khan is sleeping and he wakes up slowly when he hears the noise. The buffaloes are running towards him. He starts running down the ravine, but he is heavy with food. At the bottom of the ravine he meets the cows. He falls under the feet of the buffaloes and they run over him.

Mowgli jumps off Rama's back, runs towards the tiger and shouts, 'Shere Khan's dead! He's dead!' He takes his knife and starts cutting the coat from Shere Khan's body. It is hard work. The village hunter, Buldeo, sees Shere Khan's coat and thinks, 'I want that tiger coat.' He goes to talk to Mowgli.

'Go and look after your cows,' he says. 'The tiger coat is mine. I'm the village hunter. I can sell it for a lot of money.'

'No,' cries Mowgli, 'Don't touch this coat!'

THE JUNGLE BOOK

'Listen, boy...' says Buldeo. Suddenly Akela jumps on him and he is on the ground with a big grey wolf on top of him.

'Now go back to the village, Buldeo!' says Mowgli. Buldeo is afraid and goes away.

That evening Mowgli goes back to the village and sees the people at the gate.

'Go away, wolf child, jungle boy!' they shout. 'We don't want you here!' They start throwing stones at him.

Mowgli doesn't understand. 'Shere Khan kills their cows and takes their children,' he thinks. 'But the people of the village are angry with me. They're like the bad young wolves of the Pack.'

He looks at the stars in the night sky and says, 'I don't want to sleep in houses any more.' He turns to Akela and says, 'Let's take Shere Khan's coat and go away!'

Mowgli and the two wolves go to Mother Wolf's cave.

'The people of the village don't want me, Mother,' says Mowgli. 'This is my home! I want to stay here. And this is Shere Khan's coat!' Mother Wolf is very happy.

Bagheera comes to the cave and says, 'We're happy to see you, Little Brother.' Mowgli takes Shere Khan's coat and puts it on Council Rock. Akela sits on it and says 'Look carefully, wolves! Shere Khan is dead.'

'Now I don't belong to the Wolf Pack or to the Man Pack,' says Mowgli. 'But I can hunt alone in the jungle.'

'We can hunt with you!' say Grey Brother and the other cubs.

Mowgli returns to the jungle, and lives and hunts with his brothers.

UNDERSTANDING THE TEXT

1 COMPREHENSION CHECK

Read these sentences about Chapter Eight. Choose the correct answer (A, B or C).

1 Why do the boys run away?
   - A ☐ They are scared of people from the jungle.
   - B ☐ They think Mowgli is a wolf.
   - C ☐ Mowgli opens his mouth.

2 Where does the woman take Mowgli?
   - A ☐ back to the jungle
   - B ☐ to her friend in the village
   - C ☐ to her house

3 How do they catch Shere Khan?
   - A ☐ The buffaloes run after him into the ravine.
   - B ☐ Akela follows him into the ravine.
   - C ☐ Grey Brother chases him into the ravine.

4 What does Buldeo want?
   - A ☐ Akela's coat
   - B ☐ Mowgli
   - C ☐ Shere Khan's coat

5 Where does Mowgli put Shere Khan's coat?
   - A ☐ He puts it on top of Council Rock.
   - B ☐ He leaves it in the ravine.
   - C ☐ He takes it back to the jungle.

6 What happens to Mowgli?
   - A ☐ He returns to the village.
   - B ☐ He returns to the jungle.
   - C ☐ He becomes the leader of the wolf pack.

2 FILL IN THE GAPS

Complete this short letter from Mowgli to Messua. Write one word for each space (1-8). There is an example at the beginning (0).

Dear Messua,
Thank you (0) ..for.... your help, (1) ………… I want (2) ……… stay in the jungle (3) ………. my friends. I have a (4) ………of friends here (5) ………. we play all day together. I (6) …….. happy (7) …….. the jungle. I hope to see (8) ………… soon.
Love,
Mowgli

India

This story takes place in India. It is a very big country with almost one billion people!
The name India comes from the Indus River.
Here is some more information about India.

Capital city: New Delhi
Size: 3,287,590 square kilometres
Important cities: New Delhi, Kolkata, Ahmedabad, Chennai, Mumbai, Varanasi, Bangalore, Kanpur, Hyderabad
Important rivers: Ganges, Indus, Godavari

Indian Flag:

The old town of New Delhi.

Victoria Station, Mumbai.

The Ganges River, Varanasi.

Victoria Memorial, Kolkata.

1 COMPREHENSION CHECK
Choose the correct answer (A, B or C).

1 How many people live in India?
   - A ☐ one million
   - B ☐ two billion
   - C ☐ one billion

2 What is the name of an important river in India?
   - A ☐ Indian River
   - B ☐ Indus River
   - C ☐ Narbada River

3 What is the capital city of India?
   - A ☐ New Delhi
   - B ☐ Kolkata
   - C ☐ Mumbai

4 What are the colours of the Indian flag?
   - A ☐ yellow, white and green
   - B ☐ green and white
   - C ☐ orange, green and white

PROJECT ON THE WEB

Connect to the Internet and go to www.blackcat-cideb.com or www.cideb.it. Insert the title or part of the title of the book into our search engine.

There are a lot of wild animals in India. Some of them live in national parks. Let's take a look at them.

Work in with a partner and click on each group of wild animals. Then answer these questions:

1 Where can you find the:
   - A Indian Python?
   - B lion?
   - C leopard?
   - D jungle cat?
   - E wild buffalo?
   - F brown bear?
   - G stripped hyena?
   - H wolf?
   - I desert fox?
   - J red flying squirrel?

2 What is your favourite wild animal?

EXIT TEST

1 SNAKES AND LADDERS

On the next pages you will find the board game and the instructions. Here are the questions for the numbers on each square.

1. What type of animal is Tabaqui?
2. Who hunts in the area of the wolves?
3. Who looks after Mowgli?
4. What do the animals call a human baby?
5. What law do the animals follow?
6. Where do the wolves meet?
7. Who eats nuts and honey?
8. What colour is Bagheera?
9. What does Bagheera give the wolves to save Mowgli?
10. Who teaches Mowgli?
11. Mowgli learns some important words. What are they called?
12. What do the monkeys do all day?
13. Who does not follow the Law of the Jungle?
14. Where do the monkeys take Mowgli?
15. Who is Rann?
16. Who do Mowgli and Bagheera go with to the Lost City?
17. What type of snake is Kaa?
18. What is on a hill in the Lost City?
19. Why do the monkeys forget to bring Mowgli some food?
20. Mowgli hears, 'Your feet hurt us.' Where is he?
21. Who are the 'Poison People'?
22. What are the monkeys afraid of?
23. What is Kaa's dance called?
24. Why is Kaa's dance dangerous?
25. Why do Baloo and Bagheera punish Mowgli?
26. What do the animals call 'fire'?
27. Why do the young wolves want to kill Mowgli?
28. Where does Mowgli keep his fire?
29. What is the name of the old leader of the wolves?
30. What are the wolves and Shere Khan afraid of?
31. Mowgli asks, 'Am I dying?' What is happening?
32. What does Mowgli promise to bring the wolves?
33. Who gives Mowgli food in the village?
34. Where does Shere Khan go to hide?
35. Does Mowgli kill Shere Khan?
36. Where does Mowgli go to live at the end of the story?

Throw the dice  .

Move the same number of squares (e.g., 3).
Look at the number on the square. Another student must ask you the question with the same number on page 77.
Follow the instructions on the next page.

1 If you are at the bottom of a ladder you can climb the ladder if you answer the question correctly.
2 If you are on a snake's head and you do not answer the question correctly, you must go to the square at the end of its tail.
3 If you are on a square with one of the characters, you can throw the dice again if you answer the question correctly.

This reader uses the **EXPANSIVE READING** approach, where the text becomes a springboard to improve language skills and to explore historical background, cultural connections and other topics suggested by the text.

The new structures introduced in this step of our **GREEN APPLE** series are listed below. Naturally, structures from lower steps are included too. For a complete list of structures used over all the three steps, see *The Black Cat Guide to Graded Readers*, which is also downloadable at no cost from our website blackcat-cideb.com.

The vocabulary used at each step is carefully checked against vocabulary lists used for internationally recognised examinations.

Starter A1

Verb tenses
Present Simple
Present Continuous
Future reference: Present Continuous; *going to*;
  Present Simple

Verb forms and patterns
Affirmative, negative, interrogative
Short answers
Imperative: 2nd person; *let's*
Infinitives after some very common verbs (e.g. *want*)
Gerunds (verb + *-ing*) after some very common verbs
  (e.g. *like*, *hate*)

Modal verbs
Can: ability; requests; permission
Would ... like: offers, requests
Shall: suggestions; offers
Must: personal obligation
Have (got) to: external obligation
Need: necessity

Types of clause
Co-ordination: *but*; *and*; *or*; *and then*
Subordination (in the Present Simple or Present
  Continuous) after verbs such as: *to be sure*; *to know*;
  to think; *to believe*; *to hope*, *to say*; *to tell*
Subordination after: *because*, *when*

Other
Zero, definite and indefinite articles
Possessive *'s* and *s'*
Countable and uncountable nouns
Some, any; *much, many, a lot*; *(a) little, (a) few*;
  all, every; etc.
Order of adjectives

Available at **Starter**:

- **Alice's Adventures in Wonderland**
  Lewis Carroll
- **Bathsheba the Witch** Jane Cammack
- **Beauty and the Beast**
  Jeanne Marie Leprince de Beaumont
- **Black Beauty** Anna Sewell
- **Five Children and It** E. Nesbit
- **The Ghost Ship of Bodega Bay**
  Gina D. B. Clemen
- **Halloween Horror** Gina D. B. Clemen
- **The Happy Prince and
  The Selfish Giant** Oscar Wilde
- **The Jungle Book** Rudyard Kipling
- **The Nutcracker** E. T. A. Hoffman
- **Peter Pan** J. M. Barrie
- **Sandokan** Emilio Salgari
- **The Secret Garden**
  Frances Hodgson Burnett
- **The Secret of the Stones**
  Victoria Heward
- **The Tempest** William Shakespeare
- **The Wind in the Willows**
  Kenneth Grahame
- **The Wonderful Wizard of Oz**
  L. Frank Baum
- **Zorro!** Johnston McCulley

KEY TO EXIT TEST

1 a jackal; 2 Shere Khan; 3 The wolves/mother wolf; 4 a man cub; 5 The Law of the Jungle; 6 at Council Rock; 7 Baloo; 8 black; 9 a bull; 10 Bagheera and Baloo; 11 The Master Words; 12 they play; 13 the monkeys; 14 to the Lost City; 15 a bird; 16 Kaa, the snake; 17 a python; 18 an old palace; 19 because they are fighting; 20 In a room full of snakes; 21 the snakes; 22 water; 23 the Hunger Dance; 24 it is magical and you can walk into his mouth; 25 for talking to the monkeys; 26 the Red Flower; 27 because he's a man; 28 in a fire pot; 29 Akela; 30 fire; 31 he is crying; 32 Shere Khan's coat; 33 a woman called Messua; 34 in a big ravine; 35 no, the buffalos kill him; 36 in the jungle.

Ex. 6, Ch. 7: 1 C; 2 B; 3 A; 4 C; 5 B.